Congressional Research Service

Community Development Financial Institutions (CDFI) Fund: Programs and Policy Issues

Sean Lowry
Analyst in Public Finance

October 3, 2012

Congressional Research Service

7-5700

www.crs.gov

R42770

CRS Report for Congress ————————————————————
Prepared for Members and Committees of Congress

Summary

As communities face a variety of economic challenges, some are looking to local banks and financial institutions for solutions that address the specific development needs of low-income and distressed communities. Community development financial institutions (CDFIs) provide financial products and services, such as mortgage financing for homebuyers and not-for-profit developers, underwriting and risk capital for community facilities; technical assistance; and commercial loans and investments to small, start-up, or expanding businesses. CDFIs include regulated institutions, such as community development banks and credit unions, and non-regulated institutions, such as loan and venture capital funds.

The Community Development Financial Institutions Fund (the Fund), an agency within the Department of the Treasury, administers several programs that encourage the role of CDFIs, and similar organizations, in community development. Nearly 1,000 financial institutions located throughout all 50 states are eligible for the Fund's programs to provide financial and technical assistance to meet the needs of businesses, homebuyers, community developers, and investors in distressed communities. In addition, the Fund allocates the New Markets Tax Credit to more than 5,000 eligible investment vehicles in low-income communities (LICs).

This report begins by describing the Fund's history, current appropriations, and each of its programs. A description of the Fund's process of certifying certain financial institutions to be eligible for the Fund's program awards follows. The next section provides an overview of each program's purpose, use of award proceeds, eligibility criteria, and relevant issues for Congress.

The final section analyzes four policy considerations of congressional interest, regarding the Fund and the effective use of federal resources to promote economic development. First, it analyzes the debate on targeting development assistance toward particular geographic areas or low-income individuals generally. Prior research indicates that geographically targeted assistance, like the Fund's programs, may increase economic activity in the targeted place or area. However, this increase may be due to a shift in activity from an area not eligible for assistance.

Second, it analyzes the debate over targeting economic development policies toward labor or capital. The Fund's programs primarily rely on the latter, such as encouraging lending to small businesses, rather than targeting labor, such as wage subsidies. Research indicates the benefits of policies that reduce capital costs in a targeted place may not be passed on to local laborers, in the form of higher wages or increased employment.

Third, it examines whether the Fund plays a unique role in promoting economic development, or if it duplicates, compliments, or competes with the goals and activities of other federal, state, and local programs. Although CDFIs are eligible for other federal assistance programs and other agencies have a similar mission as the Fund, the Fund's programs have a particular emphasis on encouraging private investment and building the capacity of private financial entities to enhance local economic development

Fourth, it examines assessments of the Fund's management. Some argue that the Fund's programs are not managed in an effective manner and are not held to appropriate performance measures. Others argue that the Fund is fulfilling its mission and achieving its performance measures.

Contents

Introduction.. 1

CDFI and CDE Certification 4

Programs... 6

    CDFI Program 7

        Native American CDFI Assistance.. 10

        Small and Emerging CDFI Assistance 11

        Capacity Building Initiative 12

        Healthy Food Financing Initiative.. 12

    New Markets Tax Credit... 13

    Bank Enterprise Award 15

    Bond Guarantee Program 17

    Bank on USA... 18

Policy Considerations 18

    How Effective Are Geographically Targeted Economic Development Policies?.................... 19

    Should Economic Development Policies Target Capital or Labor? 22

    Do the Fund's Programs Duplicate Other Government Efforts?.. 23

    Is the Fund Managed Effectively?... 24

Figures

Figure 1. Certified CDFIs, by location 5

Figure 2. Certified CDEs, by location 6

Tables

Table 1. Community Development Financial Institutions (CDFI) Fund Programs
Funding, FY2012 Enacted and FY2013 Request 3

Table 2. Eligibility Criteria for CDFI and CDE Certification... 4

Table B-1. Certified Native CDFIs, by State 29

Appendixes

Appendix A. Inactive programs 27

Appendix B. Certified Native CDFIs 29

Contacts

Author Contact Information... 29

Introduction

Community development financial institutions (CDFIs) have been using small-scale, and locally developed strategies to stabilize and advance low-income and financially underserved communities for decades. CDFIs are specialized financial institutions that work in market niches that are underserved by traditional financial institutions. They provide a range of financial products and services in economically distressed markets, such as mortgage financing for low-income and first-time homebuyers and not-for-profit developers, flexible underwriting and risk capital for needed community facilities, technical assistance, and commercial loans and investments to small start-up or expanding businesses in low-income areas. CDFIs exist in both rural and urban communities. CDFIs include regulated institutions, such as community development banks and credit unions, and non-regulated institutions, such as loan and venture capital funds.

Community banks also play a role in economic recovery. The success of these banks is often linked with local communities; businesses and individuals need the financial services that community banks provide, while the banks need opportunities for profitable lending.[1] Some are specifically concerned that a shortage of credit from community banks will reduce the abilities for new entrepreneurs to establish a business, existing businesses to expand and hire new workers, and for consumers to acquire the credit they need to buy or make improvements to a property.

This report begins by describing the Community Development Financial Institutions Fund's (Fund's) history, current appropriations, and each of its programs. The next section of the report analyzes four policy considerations of congressional interest, regarding the Fund and the effective use of federal resources to promote economic

---

Types of CDFIs

- *Depository institutions* offer a range of consumer and institutional savings, checking, and lending services. This group includes for-profit community development banks and non-profit community development credit unions. These CDFIS are regulated and insured by the same agencies that govern other banks and credit unions.

- *Loan funds* are non-regulated, non-profit institutions that focus on one or more aspects of capital access and community development, such as small business lending, home mortgage financing, and community facilities development financing.

- *Community development venture capital funds* are for-profit or non-profit institutions that deliver equity capital to businesses in distressed communities.

- *Community development intermediaries* facilitate various revitalization activities between large investors and a defined population of community development corporations, CDFIs, or non-profit organizations.

Source: Federal Reserve Bank of Richmond, "Community Development Financial Institutions: A Unique Partnership for Banks," *Community Development Special Issue,* 2011.

---

development. It analyzes the reasons why some individuals may choose not to locate in an underdeveloped community, why government policies may be justified to encourage economic activity to relocate to underdeveloped communities, and which policies are more successful in addressing aspects of underdevelopment. Lastly, this report examines the Fund's programs and management to see if they represent an effective and efficient government effort to promote economic development in low-income and distressed communities.

---

[1] Ben S. Bernanke, "Community Banking," Speech at the Independent Community Bankers of America National Convention and Techworld, Nashville, TN, March 14, 2012, at http://www.federalreserve.gov/newsevents/speech/bernanke20120314a.htm.

The Riegle Community Development and Regulatory Improvement Act of 1994 (P.L. 103-325) established the Community Development Financial Institutions Fund to assist CDFIs in providing coordinated development strategies across various sectors of the local economy. These coordinated development strategies are designed to encourage small businesses, affordable housing, the availability of commercial real estate, and human development.[2] The legislation intended to improve the supply of capital, credit, private investment, and development services in economically distressed areas. In proposing the Fund, President Clinton stated that, "by ensuring greater access to capital and credit, we will tap the entrepreneurial energy of America's poorest communities and enable individuals and communities to become self-sufficient."[3]

Though the Riegle Act created the Fund as a wholly owned, independent government corporation, a supplemental appropriations bill moved the Fund into the Department of Treasury (Treasury) in 1995.[4] The Fund was moved within Treasury because of its focus on financial institutions and because other bank regulatory agencies (i.e., the Office of Thrift Supervision and Office of the Comptroller of the Currency) were already located within the agency.[5] The Fund is a component of the programs of the Under Secretary's Office of Domestic Finance, and it is directly under the Assistant Secretary for Financial Institutions.[6]

The Fund is headed by a director, who is appointed by the Secretary of the Treasury and not subject to Senate confirmation. Initially, the director served a three-year term, however the Fund was led by approximately 10 directors in its first 15 years. To bring greater stability to the Fund's leadership, the Secretary of the Treasury made the director's position into a career appointment in 2010, meaning that there are no limits on the length of the director's term.[7]

By statute, the Fund also has a 15-member Community Development Advisory Board. The board members include the Secretaries of Agriculture, Commerce, Housing and Urban Development (HUD), Interior, Treasury, the Administrator of the Small Business Administration (SBA), and nine private citizens appointed by the President. The Advisory Board's function is to advise the director of the Fund on the policies regarding the Fund's activities. The Advisory Board is not allowed, by law, to advise the Fund on the granting or denial of any particular application for monetary or non-monetary awards.

Although the Fund is organized within Treasury's Office of Domestic Finance, in recent years Congress has provided the Fund with its own budget authority line in annual financial services

---

[2] U.S. Congress, House Committee on Banking, Finance, and Urban Affairs, *Proposed Legislation: The Community Development Banking and Financial Institutions Act of 1993, Message from the President*, 103rd Cong., 1st sess., July 15, 1993, H. Doc. 103-118 (Washington: GPO, 1993).

[3] Ibid.

[4] The Emergency Supplemental Appropriations for Additional Disaster Assistance, for Anti-terrorism Initiatives, for Assistance in the Recovery from the Tragedy that Occurred at Oklahoma City, and Rescissions Act, 1995 (P.L. 104-19).

[5] See Lehn Benjamin, Julia Sass Rubin, and Sean Zielenbach, "Community Development Financial Institutions: Current Issues and Future Prospects," Proceedings, Board of Governors of the Federal Reserve System's Community Affairs Research Conference, *Sustainable Community Development: What Works, What Doesn't, and Why*, March 28, 2003, p. 7, at http://www.federalreserve.gov/communityaffairs/national/CA_Conf_SusCommDev/pdf/zeilenbachsean.pdf.

[6] U.S. Department of the Treasury, "Organizational Structure," August 11, 2011, at http://www.treasury.gov/about/organizational-structure/Pages/default.aspx.

[7] Donna Gambrell was appointed to a three-year term as the Fund's director, which began in November 2007 and expired at the end of 2010. However, Ms. Gambrell has stayed on as director under Treasury's new rules.

appropriations bills.[8] These appropriations go toward the administration of the Fund, its programs, and program awards. The Fund's appropriations cover administration of approvals for allocations of the New Markets Tax Credit (NMTC); however, the actual tax credit is awarded through the Internal Revenue Code, not through the Fund's appropriations.

As shown in **Table 1**, the Fund's enacted budget authority for FY2012 is $221 million. Of this $221 million, 66.1% (approximately $146 million) appropriated for the Fund's core CDFI assistance programs; 10.4% (approximately $23 million) appropriated for administration of the Fund's programs, including the NMTC; and the remaining 23.5% ($52 million) appropriated for set-asides for other, specific programs. For FY2012, the Fund has awarded approximately $187 million to 210 organizations in 41 states.[9]

Table 1. Community Development Financial Institutions (CDFI) Fund Programs Funding, FY2012 Enacted and FY2013 Request

(in millions of dollars)

Budget Activity	FY2012 Enacted	FY2013 Request
CDFI Program	$146,035	$127,953
Administration	22,965	21,047
Healthy Food Financing Initiative	22	25
Bank Enterprise Award Program	18	15
Native American CDFI Assistance	12	12
Bank on USA Program	NA	20
Total Budget Authority	$221	$221

Source: Community Development Financial Institutions Fund, *FY2013 President's Budget Submission*, Washington, DC, p.3, at http://www.treasury.gov/about/budget-performance/Documents/7%20-%20FY%202013%20CDFI%20CJ.pdf.

Note: Administration costs include administration of the New Markets Tax Credit.

As shown in **Table 1**, the Obama Administration's budget request for FY2013 is the same amount ($221 million) enacted for the Fund for FY2012. However, the Administration has requested somewhat higher levels of funding for the Healthy Food Financing Initiative, as well as an initial appropriation of $20.0 million for the Bank on USA program.[10] The Administration has requested that the additional funding for these programs come from the share of funding previously allocated to the CDFI program and Fund's administration.

---

[8] During the Clinton administration, funding was provided through the annual Veteran's Affairs-HUD-Independent agencies appropriations.

[9] Community Development Financial Institutions Fund, "Treasury Announces More Than $186 Million in Awards to Organizations Serving Low-Income and Native Communities," press release, August 6, 2012, at http://www.cdfifund.gov/%5Cnews_events%5CCDFI-2012-29-Treasury_Announces_More_Than_$186_Million_in_Awards_to_Organizations_Serving_Low-Income_and_Native_Communities.asp.

[10] Community Development Financial Institutions Fund, *FY 2013 President's Budget Submission*, at http://www.treasury.gov/about/budget-performance/Documents/7%20-%20FY%202013%20CDFI%20CJ.pdf.

CDFI and CDE Certification

To be eligible for certain Fund-related programs, an organization must be certified as either a CDFI or a Community Development Entity (CDE). CDFI certification is a designation conferred by the CDFI Fund and is a requirement for accessing financial award assistance from the CDFI Fund through the CDFI program, Native American CDFI Assistance (NACA) programs, and certain benefits under the Bank Enterprise Award (BEA) program to support an organization's established community development financing programs.

An organization that does not meet each of the certification eligibility requirements at the time of application for Technical Assistance is still eligible to apply for and receive Technical Assistance. This may occur if the Fund determines that the organization's application materials provide a realistic course of action to ensure that it will meet each of the certification requirements within two years of entering into an assistance agreement with the Fund.

A certified CDE is a domestic corporation or partnership that is an intermediary vehicle for the provision of loans, investments, or financial counseling in low-income communities (LICs).

Table 2. Eligibility Criteria for CDFI and CDE Certification

CDFI Certification	CDE Certification
• Be a legal entity	• Be a legal entity and a domestic corporation or partnership for federal tax purposes
• Have a primary mission of promoting community development	
• Primarily provide financial products, development services, or other similar financing in arms-length transactions	• Have a primary mission of serving or providing investment capital to low-income communities or low-income individuals and target at least 60% of activities to these groups
• Primarily serve (direct at least 60% of financial product activities to) one or more geographic investment areas meeting certain poverty or income standards; low-income targeted populations; or other targeted populations that lack adequate access to capital and historically have been denied credit	• Maintain accountability to low-income communities through representation on governing or advisory board
	• Note: Certified CDFIs qualify as CDEs and only need to register as CDEs rather than apply for certification.
• Provide development services, such as credit or homebuying counseling, in conjunction with financial products	
• Maintain accountability to defined target markets through representation on governing or advisory board or through outreach activities	
• Be a nongovernment entity and not under control of any government entity (except tribal governments)	

Source: Adopted from U.S. Government Accountability Office, *Community Development Financial Institutions and New Markets Tax Credit Programs in Metropolitan and Nonmetropolitan Areas*, GAO-12-547R, April 26, 2012, p. 4, at http://www.gao.gov/products/GAO-12-547R.

CDE certification is required to receive an NMTC allocation. CDEs use the NMTC to encourage investors to make equity investments in the CDE or its subsidiaries.[11] **Table 2** provides the eligibility criteria for CDFI and CDE certification.

Figure 1. Certified CDFIs, by location

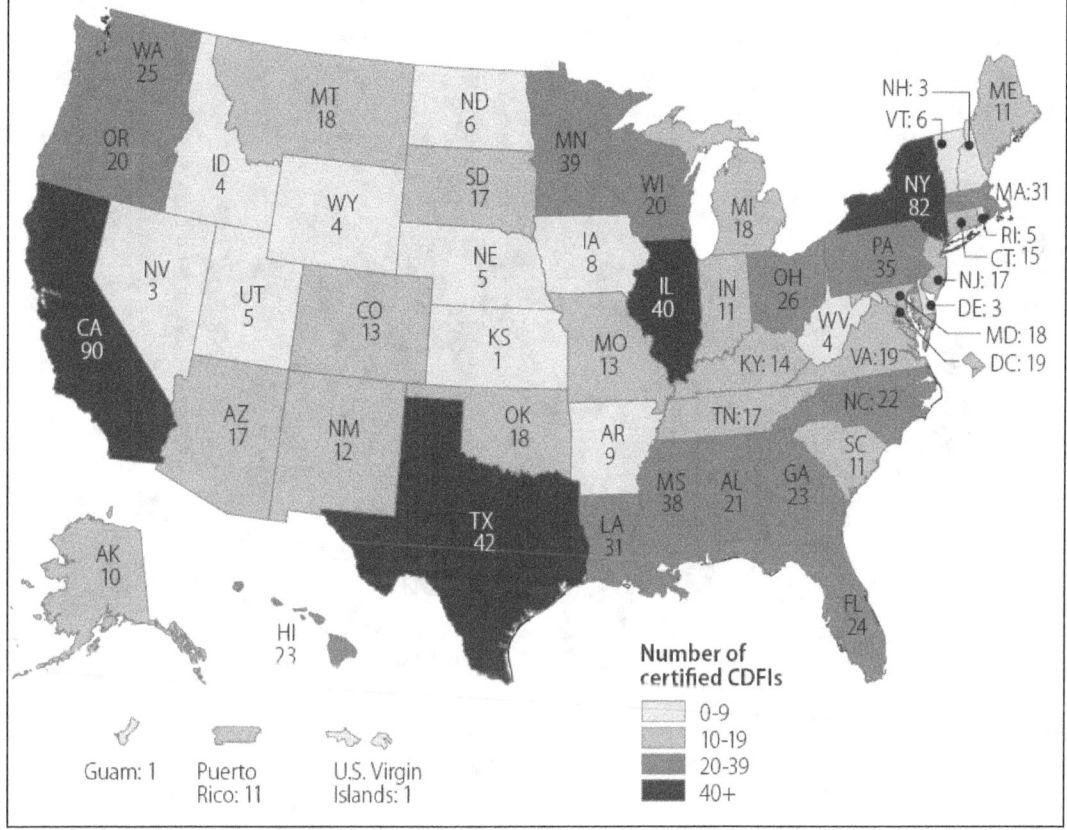

Source: Community Development Financial Institutions Fund, at http://www.cdfifund.gov/docs/certification/cdfi/ CDFI%20List%20-%2007-31-12.xls

Note: CDFI counts are as of July 31, 2012.

As of July 31, 2012, there were 999 certified CDFIs.[12] As shown in **Figure 1**, at least one CDFI is located in each of the 50 states, the District of Columbia, Guam, Puerto Rico, and the U.S. Virgin Islands. California and New York contain more certified CDFIs than any other U.S. state or territory.

---

[11] Community Development Financial Institutions Fund, "CDE Certification," at http://www.cdfifund.gov/ what_we_do/programs_id.asp?programID=10.

[12] For a list of these certified CDFIs with their contact information, see Community Development Financial Institutions Fund, "CDFI Certification," at http://www.cdfifund.gov/what_we_do/programs_id.asp?programID=9.

As of July 31, 2012, there were 5,780 certified CDEs (including their subsidiaries) located throughout the United States, Puerto Rico, and the U.S. Virgin Islands.[13] As shown in **Figure 2**, California and New York also contain more certified CDEs than any other U.S. state or territory.

Figure 2. Certified CDEs, by location

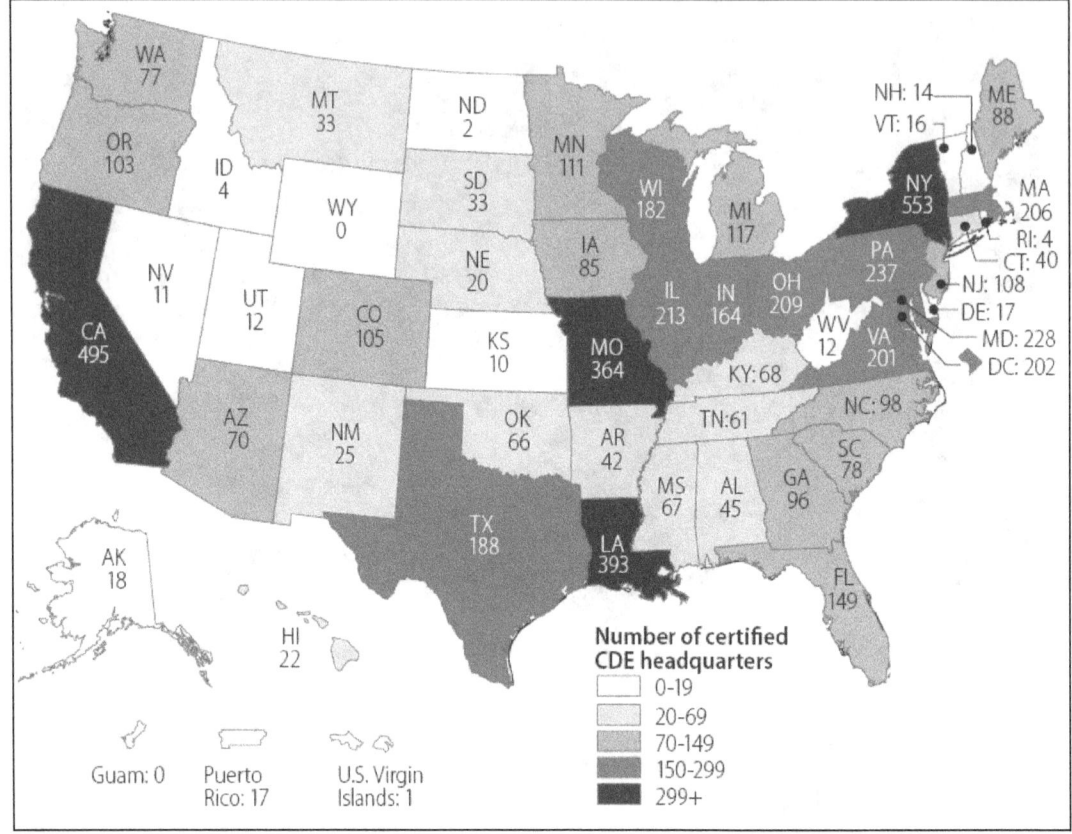

Source: Community Development Financial Institutions Fund, at http://www.cdfifund.gov/what_we_do/programs_id.asp?programID=10.

Note: CDE counts are as of July 31, 2012.

Programs

The Fund's official mission is to increase economic opportunity and promote community development investments in low-income and distressed communities in the United States. To carry out this mission, the Fund is composed of several programs that address multiple needs of distressed communities. These programs encourage qualified entities to provide financial and technical assistance to meet the needs of local businesses, potential homebuyers, community developers, and potential investors in distressed and LICs. The Fund's range of incentives include

---

[13] For a list of these certified CDEs (and their subsidiaries) with their contact information, see Community Development Financial Institutions Fund, "CDE Certification," at http://www.cdfifund.gov/what_we_do/programs_id.asp?programID=10.

equity investment in program awardees, tax credits, grants, loans, and deposits and credit union shares in insured CDFIs and state-insured credit unions.[14]

All of the Fund's programs share a common characteristic, in that they use geographically targeted incentives intended to increase community development in underserved and distressed communities, where certain types of economic activity might not otherwise occur. Ideas for geographically targeted community development policies were a feature of federal policy debates throughout the 1980s and early 1990s.[15] Despite bipartisan support for these policies at the time, they did not become more widely implemented, at the federal level, until the Clinton Administration.[16]

According to the Fund, it has awarded (as of the end of FY2010) $1.3 billion to CDFIs, community development organizations, and financial institutions through its core CDFI assistance program (and component initiatives) and the BEA program since the Fund's founding in 1994.[17] The Fund has also allocated $26 billion in tax credit authority to certified CDEs through the New Markets Tax Credit, between 2001 and 2010.

By the Fund's estimates, CDFIs that received the Fund's awards, in FY2011 alone, created or maintained more than 25,000 jobs, opened more than 6,500 bank accounts for the previously unbanked, and provided more than 177,000 individuals with financial literacy training.[18] The Fund's Community Investment Impact System, launched in 2004, contains these statistics gathered through reporting requirements that are part of the terms of each program's award agreements.[19]

CDFI Program

The Fund's core CDFI program was authorized by the Community Development Banking and Financial Institutions Act of 1994 in the Riegle Community Development and Regulatory Improvement Act of 1994 (P.L. 103-325). The CDFI program provides two types of monetary awards, financial assistance (FA) and technical assistance (TA). These awards are given to CDFIs to build their capacity of CDFIs to serve low-income people and communities that lack access to affordable financial products and services.[20]

To be eligible for an FA award, a CDFI must be certified by the Fund before it applies for the award. Prospective applicants that are not yet certified must submit a separate certification application to be considered for an FA award during a funding round. Both certified and non-

---

[14] 12 C.F.R. §1805.401.

[15] For a historical analysis of these debates, see the Discussion section of CRS Report R41268, *Small Business Administration HUBZone Program*, by Robert Jay Dilger.

[16] These programs include the 1993 reform of the Community Reinvestment Act of 1977 (P.L. 95-128) and the Empowerment Zone program, established by the Omnibus Budget Reconciliation Act of 1993 (P.L. 103-66).

[17] Community Development Financial Institutions Fund, *Performance and Accountability Report FY 2010*, , January 2011, p.4, at http://www.cdfifund.gov/docs/2011/cdfi/Performance-and-Accountabilty-Report-FY-2010.pdf.

[18] Community Development Financial Institutions Fund, *CDFI Program Awards FY 2012*, August 13, 2012, p. 6, at http://www.cdfifund.gov/docs/2012/cdfi/CDFI%20AWARDSbook%208%202012.pdf.

[19] Community Development Financial Institutions Fund, "Research Reports, Research Briefs and Impact Data," May 5, 2012, at http://www.cdfifund.gov/impact_we_make/data_reports.asp.

[20] Laws pertaining to the Fund's FA and TA are located in 46 U.S.C. §§1805.300-1805.303.

---

certified CDFIs are eligible to apply for TA awards. However, non-certified organizations must be able to become certified within two years after receiving a TA award.

In evaluating and selecting applicants for awards, the Fund evaluates the applicants' likelihood of meeting its goals as described in a required comprehensive business plan. The applicants' prior history of servicing distressed communities, its operational capacity, financial track record, and other attributes are also taken into consideration.[21]

Activities eligible for program awards must target a *distressed community*, which is defined by two requirements. First, the community (investment area) must meet minimum area requirements. The community must be a continuous area of general local government that either has (1) a population of at least 4,000, if located in a Metropolitan Statistical Area, (2) a population of at least 1,000, in non-metropolitan areas, or (3) located entirely within an Indian reservation.[22]

Second, at least 30% of the eligible residents in the community must have incomes that are less than the national poverty level, as published by the U.S. Bureau of Labor Statistics (BLS), and the community must have an unemployment rate that is at least 1.5 times greater than the national average, as determined by the BLS's most recent data. In addition, the Fund may specify other requirements in a program's applicable notice of funds availability (NOFA).[23] The Fund's online resource, CDFI Fund Mapping System (CIMS), designates which localities either fully qualify or partially qualify as distressed communities, based on the three criteria.[24]

If the community does not meet the individual minimum area requirements, the applicant may select two or more geographic units which, in the aggregate, meet the minimum area eligibility requirements, provided that none of the geographic units has a poverty rate less than 20%.[25]

> **Minimum Requirements for Meeting the CDFI Program's Definition of a Distressed Community:**
>
> - A contiguous area located with a unit of General Local Government with a population, as determined by the most recent census data available, of at least 4,000, if any of the portion of the area is located with a Metropolitan Area with a population of 50,000; a population of at least 1,000, in any other case; or be located entirely within an Indian reservation;
>
> - At least 30% of the Eligible Residents have incomes that are less than the national poverty level, as published by the U.S. Bureau of the Census in the most recent decennial census for which data is available; the unemployment rate is at least 1.5 times greater than the national average, as determined by the U.S. Bureau of Labor Statistics' (BLS) most recent data, including estimates of unemployment developed using the BLS's Census Share calculation method; or
>
> - Such additional requirements as may be specified by the Fund in the applicable notice of funds availability.
>
> **Source:** 12 C.F.R. §1806.200(b).

The Fund makes awards up to $2 million to certified CDFIs under the FA component of the CDFI program.[26] A CDFI may use an FA award for lending, investing, enhancing liquidity, or other means of financing:

---

[21] 12 CFR §1805.701.

[22] 12 C.F.R. §1806.200(b)(1).

[23] 12 C.F.R. §1806.200(b)(2).

[24] Community Development Financial Institutions Fund, "Community Development Financial Institutions Fund Mapping System (CIMS)," December 3, 2008, at http://www.cdfifund.gov/what_we_do/mapping.asp.

[25] 12 C.F.R. §1806.200(c).

[26] Community Development Financial Institutions Fund, "Community Development Financial Institutions Program," (continued...)

- commercial facilities that promote revitalization, community stability, or job creation or retention;

- businesses that provide jobs to, are owned by, or enhance the availability of products and services to low-income individuals;

- housing that is principally affordable to low-income persons, with some exceptions;

- the provision of consumer loans; or

- other businesses or activities as requested by the applicant and deemed appropriate by the Fund.[27]

The Fund awards grants of up $100,000 to certified CDFIs and established entities seeking to become certified under the TA component of the CDFI program. TA awards are intended to build a CDFI's capacity to provide affordable financial products and services to low-income communities and families.[28] TA grants may be used for a variety of purposes, including

- the purchase equipment, materials, or supplies;

- to pay for consulting or contracting services;

- to pay the salaries and benefits of certain personnel;

- to train staff or board members;

- or other activities deemed appropriate by the Fund.[29]

FA and TA awards are both generally subject to two restrictions. First, the Fund typically requires an applicant to demonstrate that they can match from a non-federal source, dollar-for-dollar, the amount of money that they are requesting from the Fund. With regard to FA awards, the Fund is authorized to make awards to applicants in a *like form* to the matching funds secured by the awardee.[30] For example, the Fund can only match a non-federal grant with an FA grant—not a loan. Second, the Fund generally limits any one entity or its affiliates from receiving more than $5 million in awards from the Fund within a three-year period.[31]

However, restrictions on the Fund's awards have been subject to temporary legislative changes. For example, the American Reinvestment and Recovery Act (ARRA) of 2009 (P.L. 111-5) waived the non-federal, dollar-for-dollar matching requirement for three years.[32] Thus, the Fund did not require awards in FY2009, FY2010, and FY2011 to be matched by non-federal sources.[33] The

---

(...continued)

August 6, 2012, at http://www.cdfifund.gov/what_we_do/programs_id.asp?programid=7.

[27] 12 C.F.R. §1805.301.

[28] Ibid.

[29] 12 C.F.R. §1805.303.

[30] 12 C.F.R. §1805.501.

[31] 12 C.F.R. §1805.402(a). However, an entity and its affiliates may receive up to $8.75 million in awards from the Fund within a three year period if the entity serves an area where there are no other applicants for awards. These exceptions to $5 million cap are detailed in 12 C.F.R. §§1805.402(b)-(c).

[32] American Recovery and Reinvestment Act of 2009 (P.L. 111-5), 123 Stat. 148.

[33] Ibid.

---

matching requirement returned for awards in FY2012 for Fund programs that did not receive a congressional wavier.[34] ARRA also waived the $5 million cap for FY2009, FY2010, and FY2011.[35]

Native American CDFI Assistance

The origin of the Native American CDFI Assistance (NACA) component of the CDFI program dates back to the Riegle Act of 1994. The Riegle Act mandated that the Fund conduct a study of lending and investment practices on Indian reservations. The study was directed to identify and determine the impact of private-financing barriers on Native American populations.[36] Since the November 2001 release of the Native American Lending Study, the Fund certifies Native CDFIs and provides assistance through the CDFI program's authority. These programs are designed to reduce barriers preventing access to credit, capital, and financial services in Native American, Alaska Native, and Native Hawaiian communities (collectively referred to as Native Communities).[37]

The Fund receives a separate appropriation for the NACA component of the CDFI program. Under the NACA component of the CDFI program, the Fund issues FA and TA awards to organizations with the primary mission of increasing access to capital in Native Communities. In addition, the NACA component provides TA grants to certified Native CDFIs, emerging Native CDFIs, and sponsoring entities (see below). TA awards may be used by the recipient to become certified as a Native CDFI or to create a new Native CDFI.

A CDFI must be certified by the Fund as one of three types of entities to become eligible for NACA's FA and TA awards:[38]

- *certified Native CDFI*, an organization must direct at least 50% of its activities toward serving Native Communities;

- *emerging Native CDFI*, an organization must demonstrate to the satisfaction of the Fund that is has a plan to achieve Native CDFI certification within a reasonable timeframe; or

- *sponsoring entity*, an organization (typically a tribe or tribal entity) must pledge that it will create a separate legal entity, which will eventually become certified as a Native CDFI.

---

[34] For FY 2012 funding rounds, Congress waived the matching funds requirement for Small and Emerging CDFI Assistance (SECA) program applicants and Financial Assistance (FA) applicants for the Native American CDFI Assistance (NACA) program. See Community Development Financial Institutions Fund, "Matching Funds Update for CDFI and NACA Program Applicants," press release, January 4, 2012, at http://www.cdfifund.gov/news_events/CDFI-2011-41-Matching_Funds_Funding_Cap_Update_CDFI_Program_NACA_Program_Applicants.asp.

[35] See Catalog of Federal Domestic Assistance, "Community Development Financial Institutions Program," program information, accessed August 13, 2012, at https://www.cfda.gov/?s=program&mode=form&tab=step1&id=18dd106bf98422454e41f434ed2856d8.

[36] P.L. 103-325, Section 117(c).

[37] For the results of this study, see Community Development Financial Institutions Fund, *The Report of the Native American Lending Study*, November 2001, at http://www.cdfifund.gov/docs/2001_nacta_lending_study.pdf.

[38] Community Development Financial Institutions Fund, "Native American Initiatives Program," at http://www.cdfifund.gov/what_we_do/programs_id.asp?programid=3.

For FY2012 funding rounds, Congress waived the matching funds requirement for FA applicants to the NACA program.[39]

Table B-1 summarizes the locations of Certified Native CDFIs, by state. Hawaii and Oklahoma contain more certified Native CDFIs than any other U.S. state.

As shown in **Table 1**, the Obama Administration requested $12 million for the assistance to Native CDFIs for FY2013.[40] Both the House and Senate Committee on Appropriations also recommended $12 million in assistance for Native CDFIs for FY2013.[41]

Small and Emerging CDFI Assistance

The Small and Emerging CDFI Assistance (SECA) component of the CDFI program is designed to assist small or emerging CDFIs. It provides the same type of FA and TA awards as the general CDFI program. It distinguishes small or emerging CDFIs from other CDFIs using two eligibility criteria, as announced in the annual notice of funds availability. For FY2012 awards, a certified CDFI met the eligibility criteria of being a small or emerging CDFI if they had financial holdings below certain caps (based on their respective type of financial institution), or if they began operations after January 1, 2008.[42]

Awards provided through the SECA application are subject to caps on the size of the awards. For FY2012, these caps included $600,000 in general FA funds, up to and including $3.5 million funds under the FA funds designated for the Healthy Food Financing Initiative, and up to $100,000 in TA funds for capacity-building activities.[43] For FY2012 funding rounds, Congress waived the matching funds requirement for SECA program applicants.[44]

In FY2012, 26% of the total CDFI program applicant pool was requested by CDFIs that filed under the SECA component.[45]

---

[39] Consolidated Appropriations Act, 2012 (P.L. 112-74), 125 Stat. 887.

[40] Community Development Financial Institutions Fund, *FY2013 President's Budget Submission,* , p.3, at http://www.treasury.gov/about/budget-performance/Documents/7%20-%20FY%202013%20CDFI%20CJ.pdf.

[41] U.S. Congress, House Committee on Appropriations, *Financial Services and General Government Appropriations Bill, 2013,* 112th Cong., 2nd sess., June 26, 2012, H.Rept. 112-550 (Washington: GPO, 2012), p. 16; and U.S. Congress, Senate Committee on Appropriations, *Financial Services and General Government Appropriations Bill, 2013,* 112th Cong., 2nd sess., June 14, 2012, S.Rept. 112-177 (Washington: GPO, 2012), p. 22.

[42] For FY2012, the caps for awards eligibility under SECA were set as follows: $250 million (insured depository institutions and depository institution holding companies), $10 million (insured credit unions), $10 million (venture capital funds), and $5 million (other CDFIs). See Department of the Treasury, "Community Development Financial Institutions Fund - Funds Availability (NOFA) Inviting Applications for the Community Development Financial Institutions (CDFI) Program FY 2012 Funding Round," 76 *Federal Register* 68831-68841, November 7, 2011.

[43] Ibid.

[44] Consolidated Appropriations Act, 2012 (P.L. 112-74), 125 Stat. 887.

[45] Community Development Financial Institutions Fund, "Community Development Financial Institutions Fund Releases Application Demand for the FY 2012 CDFI Program Funding Round," press release, March 1, 2012, at http://www.cdfifund.gov/news_events/CDFI-2012-02-CDFI-Fund-Releases-Application-Demand-for-the-FY-2012-CDFI-Program-Funding-Round.asp.

Capacity Building Initiative

The Fund provides technical assistance and training opportunities for CDFIs through its Capacity Building Initiative. The Capacity Building Initiative is a combination of online and in-person resources.[46] The Fund's website provides a collection of best practices related to topics, such as microfinance operations, foreclosure intervention counseling, and healthy food retail financing in low-income communities. The Fund also offers a limited number of in-person training events on similar topics in different locations across the United States.

The Senate Committee on Appropriations recommended that $2 million of its $223 million in appropriations for the Fund be designated for the Capacity Building Initiative for FY2013.[47] The House Committee on Appropriations did not designate any level of funds specifically for the initiative.[48]

Healthy Food Financing Initiative

The Fund has used its authority within its CDFI program to support the Healthy Food Financing Initiative (HFFI), which began in FY2011. The Fund's HFFI is part of a multi-agency HFFI, involving Treasury, the U.S. Department of Agriculture (USDA), and the U.S. Department of Health and Human Services (HHS).[49] The HFFI represents the federal government's effort to expand the supply and demand for nutritious foods, including increasing the distribution of agricultural products, developing and equipping grocery stores, and strengthening producer-to-consumer relationships. Through its role in the HFFI, the Fund provides grants for organizations serving low-income neighborhoods with limited access to affordable and nutritious food.

Congress appropriated $22 million for Fund activities related to the HFFI for FY2012. Twelve CDFIs focusing on developing solutions for increasing access to affordable healthy foods received grants in FY2011.[50] The Obama Administration and the Senate Committee on Appropriations recommended a $3 million increase (to $25 million) in FY2013 for the HFFI.[51] The House Committee on Appropriations did not recommend a specific level of funding for the HFFI for FY2013.[52]

---

[46] Community Development Financial Institutions Fund, "Capacity Building Initiative," March 25, 2010, at http://www.cdfifund.gov/what_we_do/programs_id.asp?programID=13.

[47] U.S. Congress, Senate Committee on Appropriations, *Financial Services and General Government Appropriations Bill, 2013*, 112th Cong., 2nd sess., June 14, 2012, S.Rept. 112-177 (Washington: GPO, 2012), p. 22.

[48] U.S. Congress, House Committee on Appropriations, *Financial Services and General Government Appropriations Bill, 2013*, 112th Cong., 2nd sess., June 26, 2012, H.Rept. 112-550 (Washington: GPO, 2012), p. 16.

[49] Community Development Financial Institutions Fund, "Community Development Financial Institutions Fund Announces $25 Million in Healthy Food Financing Initiative Awards," press release, September 14, 2011, at http://www.cdfifund.gov/news_events/CDFI-2011-18-CDFI-Fund-Announces-$25-Million-in-Healthy-Food-Financing-Initiative-Awards.asp.

[50] Community Development Financial Institutions Fund, "CDFI Fund Announces $25 Million in Healthy Food Financing Initiative Awards," press release, September 14, 2011, at http://www.cdfifund.gov/news_events/CDFI-2011-18-CDFI-Fund-Announces-$25-Million-in-Healthy-Food-Financing-Initiative-Awards.asp.

[51] U.S. Congress, Senate Committee on Appropriations, *Financial Services and General Government Appropriations Bill, 2013*, 112th Cong., 2nd sess., June 14, 2012, S.Rept. 112-177 (Washington: GPO, 2012), p. 22.

[52] U.S. Congress, House Committee on Appropriations, *Financial Services and General Government Appropriations Bill, 2013*, 112th Cong., 2nd sess., June 26, 2012, H.Rept. 112-550 (Washington: GPO, 2012), p. 16.

New Markets Tax Credit

Congress established the New Markets Tax Credit (NMTC) program as part of the Community Renewal Tax Relief Act of 2000, contained within the Consolidated Appropriations Act, 2001 (P.L. 106-554), to encourage investors to make investments in impoverished, low-income communities (LICs) that traditionally lack access to capital. The NMTC is designed to increase private investment in LICs, where conventional access to credit and investment capital for developing small businesses, creating and retaining jobs, and revitalizing neighborhoods is often limited.[53] The NMTC is a non-refundable tax credit intended to encourage qualified investment groups to support community development entities (CDEs) that operate in eligible, LICs.[54] Although the NMTC is credited through the federal tax code, the Fund is responsible for awarding the tax credit allocations to eligible CDEs through a competitive award process. The credit provided to the investor totals 39% of the amount of the investment made in a CDE and is claimed over a seven-year credit allowance period.[55] In each of the first three years, the investor receives a credit equal to 5% of the total amount paid for the stock or capital interest at the time of purchase. For the final four years, the value of the credit is 6% annually. Investors must retain their interest in a qualified equity investment throughout the seven-year period, or risk forfeiture of that interest.[56]

Under the tax code's NMTC provisions, only eligible investments in qualifying LICs can receive the NMTC. Qualifying LICs include census tracts that have at least one of the following criteria: (1) a poverty rate of at least 20%; (2) is located in a metropolitan area, a median family income below 80% of the greater of the statewide, or metropolitan area median family income; or (3) if located outside a metropolitan area, a median family income below 80% of the median statewide family income. As defined by the criteria above, about 39% of the nation's census tracts covering nearly 36% of the U.S. population are eligible for the NMTC.[57] In addition, designated targeted populations may be treated as LICs. As a result of the definition of qualified LICs, virtually all of the country's census tracts are potentially eligible for the NMTC.[58]

Qualified investment groups can apply to the Fund for an allocation of the NMTC. CDEs seek individuals who can benefit from tax preferences to make qualifying equity investments in the CDE.[59] The CDE then makes equity investments in LICs and low-income community businesses, all of which must be qualified. After the CDE is awarded a tax credit allocation, the CDE is authorized to offer the tax credits to private equity investors in the CDE.

---

[53] U.S. Government Accountability Office, *New Markets Tax Credit: The Credit Helps Fund a Variety of Projects in Low-Income Communities, but Could Be Simplified*, GAO-10-334, January 2010, p. 1, at http://www.gao.gov/new.items/d10334.pdf.

[54] A non-refundable tax credit, like the NMTC, can be used to reduce tax liability toward, but not below, zero. In contrast, a refundable tax credit can be used to reduce tax liability beyond zero, enabling a taxpayer to receive a tax refund from the Internal Revenue Service.

[55] Laws pertaining to the NMTC are located in 26 U.S.C. §45D.

[56] For more details on the NMTC, see CRS Report RL34402, *New Markets Tax Credit: An Introduction*, by Donald J. Marples.

[57] CRS Report RL34402, *New Markets Tax Credit: An Introduction*, by Donald J. Marples.

[58] Ibid.

[59] If an investor does not have a tax liability, then the investor would not benefit from the non-refundable NMTC.

The Tax Relief, Unemployment Insurance Reauthorization, and Job Creation Act of 2010 (P.L. 111-312) extended NMTC authorization through 2011 at $3.5 billion per year. The 112th Congress may choose to reinstate the NMTC. The Family and Business Tax Cut Certainty Act of 2012 (S. 3521) would extend the NMTC for calendar years 2012 and 2013, with an allocation authority of $3.5 billion per year.[60] Despite a lack guaranteed appropriations of the NMTC for 2012, the Fund issued a notice of NTMC allocation availability for 2012 on July 24, 2012.[61]

The Government Accountability Office (GAO) has issued several reports examining the NMTC's overall performance and ability to benefit certain types of LICs. A 2007 GAO report contains survey results from a sample of NMTC recipients suggesting that the NMTC influenced the decisions of investors to invest in LICs.[62] GAO published a 2009 report responding to congressional concerns about the low success rate of minority-owned CDEs in obtaining NMTC allocations. GAO found that although a CDE's resources and experience are important factors in successfully obtaining an NMTC allocation, minority status is associated with a lower probability of receiving an allocation, when controlling for other factors. GAO could not determine why this relationship exists or whether any actions (or lack of) by the Department of the Treasury contributed to minority CDEs' lower probability of success, given that the Fund provides assistance that is available to all CDEs that do not receive awards detailing some of the weaknesses in its applications.[63] In a 2012 report, GAO concluded that although the NMTC directed most awards and tax credits to metropolitan areas, it generally met proportionality goals of nonmetropolitan areas.[64] Another GAO report released in 2012 reported that the effects of the NMTC are difficult to assess because of information gaps in the collection of tax data.[65]

In addition, the NMTC's complex application and administration have been the focus of GAO reports, which have provided recommendations to make the program simpler and more accessible to those in LICs. For example, a 2010 GAO report noted that the complexity of NMTC transaction structures appears to make it more difficult for CDEs to execute smaller transactions and results in less equity ending up in low-income community businesses than would likely end up there were the transaction structures simplified.[66] In a 2011 report, GAO suggested that

---

[60] Joint Committee on Taxation, *Description of the "Family and Business Tax Cut Certainty Act of 2012"*, JCX-67-12, July 31, 2012, at http://www.finance.senate.gov/legislation/download/?id=33b9fd68-7a66-4875-a069-0d74f874bad6.

[61] Department of the Treasury, "Community Development Institutions Fund - Funding Opportunity Title: Notice of Allocation Availability (NOAA) Inviting Applications for the CY 2012 Allocation Round of the New Markets Tax Credit (NMTC) Program," 77 *Federal Register* 142, July 24, 2012.

[62] U.S. Government Accountability Office, New Markets Tax Credit Appears to Increase Investment by Investors in Low-Income Communities, but Opportunities Exist to Better Monitor Compliance, GAO-07-296, January 2007, p. 35, at http://www.gao.gov/new.items/d07296.pdf.

[63] U.S. Government Accountability Office, *New Markets Tax Credit: Minority Entities Are Less Successful in Obtaining Awards Than Non-Minority Entities*, GAO-09-536, April 2009, at http://www.gao.gov/new.items/d09536.pdf.

[64] U.S. Government Accountability Office, *Community Development Financial Institutions and New Markets Tax Credit Programs in Metropolitan and Nonmetropolitan Areas*, GAO-12-547R, April 2012, at http://www.gao.gov/assets/600/590432.pdf.

[65] U.S. Government Accountability Office, *Limited Information on the Use and Effectiveness of Tax Expenditures Could be Mitigated Through Congressional Action*, GAO-12-262, February 2012, at http://gao.gov/assets/590/588978.pdf.

[66] See U.S. Government Accountability Office, *New Markets Tax Credit: The Credit Helps Fund a Variety of Projects in Low-Income Communities, but Could Be Simplified*, GAO-10-334, January 2010, p.41, at http://www.gao.gov/new.items/d10334.pdf.

Congress convert at least part of the NMTC to a grant program to increase the amount of federal subsidy reaching businesses in impoverished, LICs.[67]

Bank Enterprise Award

The Bank Enterprise Award (BEA) was originally authorized by the Bank Enterprise Act of 1991 in the Agriculture, Rural Development, Food and Drug Administration, and Related Agencies Appropriations Act, 1992 (P.L. 102-142). Prior to the creation of the Fund, the BEA was administered by the Comptroller of the Currency and the Federal Deposit Insurance Corporation (FDIC). Section 114 of the Riegle Community Development and Regulatory Improvement Act of 1994 (P.L. 103-325) moved the BEA under the operations of the Fund.

The Fund's BEA program provides formula-based grants to FDIC-insured banks and thrifts to expand investments in CDFIs and to increase lending, investment, and service activities within economically distressed communities. The Fund measures increases in an applicant's lending, investment, and service activities relative to a baseline of similar, qualified activities conducted by the applicant in the previous application cycle. BEA rewards are *retrospective*, awarding applicants for activities they have already completed, in contrast to the Fund's primary CDFI program—which typically award applicants based on their plans for the future.[68]

The BEA provides formula-based grants to qualified banks and thrifts based on three categories:

- *CDFI-related activities* include equity investments (e.g., grants, stock purchases, purchases of partnership interests, or limited liability company membership interests), equity-like loans, and support activities (e.g., loans, deposits, or technical assistance), to certified CDFIs.[69]

- *Distressed community financing activities* include loans or investments for home mortgages, housing development, home improvement, commercial real estate development, small businesses, and education financing in distressed communities.

- *Service activities* include the provision of financial services (e.g., check-cashing or money order services, electronic transfer accounts, and individual development accounts).[70]

FDIC-insured financial institutions that are dedicated to financing and supporting economic development in qualified communities are eligible for the BEA. No applicant may receive a BEA if it has (1) an application pending for assistance under the current round of the awards under the

[67] U.S. Government Accountability Office, *Opportunities to Reduce Potential Duplication of Government Programs, Save Tax Dollars, and Enhance Revenue*, GAO-11-318SP, March 2011, at http://www.gao.gov/new.items/d11318sp.pdf.

[68] The Fund publishes a more in-depth account of its BEA application evaluation process regularly in the program's notice of funds availability. For example, see Department of Treasury, "Community Development Financial Institutions Fund - Notice of Funds Availability (NOFA) inviting Applications for the FY 2012 Funding Round of the Bank Enterprise Award (BEA) Program," 77 *Federal Register* 37742-37749, June 22, 2012.

[69] Community Development Financial Institutions Fund, "FY 2012 Funding Round of BEA Program Now Open," press release, June 30, 2012, at http://www.cdfifund.gov/news_events/CDFI-2012-24-FY_2012_Funding_Round_of_BEA_Program_Now_Open.asp.

[70] 12 C.F.R. §1806.101(3)(c).

CDFI program; (2) been awarded assistance from the Fund under the CDFI program within the 12-month period prior to the date the Fund selects the applicant to receive a BEA; or (3) ever received assistance under the CDFI program for the same activities for which it is seeking a BEA.[71] Applicants may apply for both a CDFI program award and a BEA program award in a given year; however, receiving a CDFI program award removes an applicant from eligibility for a BEA in the same year.[72]

According to a GAO report, the Fund's authorizing statute places no restrictions on how BEA recipients may use their award.[73] In this same report, the Fund agreed with GAO's interpretation of its authorizing statute.[74] However, the Fund changed the terms of the program's award agreements in 2009.[75] Recipients must now use the award, or an amount equivalent to the award amount, for BEA qualified activities in a distressed community.[76] This change in the BEA program generated public requests for the Fund to provide further guidance on an awardee's reporting requirements.[77] As part of the BEA award agreement, the Fund now requires BEA recipients to account and track the use of the award (or an amount equivalent to the award amount) and verify that this amount was used in accordance with performance goals designated by the Fund.

As shown in **Table 1**, the Obama Administration recommended that the BEA program receive $15 million for FY2013.[78] Neither the House or Senate Committee on Appropriations recommended a specific level of funding for the BEA program for FY2013.

The BEA program's effect on investment in distressed communities is the topic of multiple GAO reports to Congress. In 1998, GAO reported that, according to the Fund, most of the 1996 awardees reported using their awards to further the objectives of the BEA program even though the program's authorizing legislation did not place restrictions on the use of the awards.[79] Each of GAO's five case study banks also reported using its award money to expand its existing investments in community development.[80] In a 2006 report, GAO concluded that the extent to which the BEA program may provide banks with incentives to increase their investments in CDFIs and lending in distressed communities is difficult to determine, but available evidence GAO reviewed suggested that the program's impact has likely not been significant. Award recipients GAO

---

[71] 12 C.F.R. §1805.102, and U.S. Department of the Treasury, "Community Development Financial Institutions Fund - Notice of Funds Availability (NOFA) inviting Applications for the FY 2012 Funding Round of the Bank Enterprise Award (BEA) Program," 77 *Federal Register* 37743, June 22, 2012.

[72] Ibid.

[73] U.S. Government Accountability Office, Treasury's Bank Enterprise Award Program: Impact on Investments in Distressed Communities Is Difficult to Determine, but Likely Not Significant, GAO-06-824, July 2006, p. 6, at http://www.gao.gov/new.items/d06824.pdf.

[74] Ibid., p.28.

[75] Department of the Treasury, "Community Development Financial Institutions Fund 12 CFR Part 1806," 74 *Federal Register* 5790, January 30, 2009.

[76] 12 C.F.R. §1806.101(c).

[77] Letter from Joseph Pigg, Vice President and Senior Counsel, to Jodie Harris, Associate Program Manager - Community Development Financial Institutions Fund, March 24, 2010, at http://www.aba.com/Issues/Documents/c7e6303e475b4085afef85855eb422f632410TreasuryBankEnterpriseAwardProgramBEA.pdf.

[78] Community Development Financial Institutions Fund, *FY2013 President's Budget Submission*, p. 3, at http://www.treasury.gov/about/budget-performance/Documents/7%20-%20FY%202013%20CDFI%20CJ.pdf.

[79] Ibid.

[80] Ibid., p.54.

interviewed said that the BEA program lowers bank costs associated with investing in a CDFI or lending in a distressed community, allowing for increases in both types of activities. However, other economic and regulatory incentives also encourage banks to undertake award-eligible activities, and it is difficult to isolate and distinguish these incentives from those of a BEA award.[81] Treasury disputed GAO's findings and questioned GAO's methodology of evaluating the BEA program.

Bond Guarantee Program

The Small Business Jobs Act of 2010 (P.L. 111-240) authorized the Bond Guarantee program on September 27, 2010.[82] The Fund's Bond Guarantee program is designed to provide a low-cost source of long-term, patient capital to CDFIs.[83] Treasury may issue up to 10 bonds per year, each at a minimum of $100 million. The total of all bonds cannot exceed $1 billion per year. Each bond is fully guaranteed by the United States and offered at a cost equivalent to the current Treasury rates for comparable maturities. The bonds cannot exceed a maturity of 30 years, are taxable, and do not qualify for Community Reinvestment Act (CRA) credit.[84] Treasury guarantees the full amount of notes or bonds issued to support CDFIs that make investments for eligible community or economic development purposes.[85]

Authorized uses of the loans financed may include a variety of financial activities that constitute community or economic development in low-income or underserved areas (e.g., the provision of basic financial services, housing that is principally affordable to low-income individuals, and businesses that provide jobs for low-income people or are owned by low-income individuals).[86]

By legislative design, the Bond Guarantee program is a zero subsidy credit program and does not require annual appropriations funding. Since the bonds will be guaranteed by the United States, in accordance with federal credit policy, the Federal Financing Bank (FFB), a U.S. government corporation under the general supervision and direction of Treasury, will purchase the bonds issued by qualified issuers.[87] Qualified issuers will lend the bond proceeds to eligible CDFIs. The FFB finances obligations that are fully guaranteed by the United States, such as the bonds or notes issued by CDFIs under the CDFI Bond Guarantee Program.

The Fund has not yet published regulations concerning the eligibility criteria for its Bond Guarantee program, as of the publication date of this report.

Although the Bond Guarantee program is authorized through FY2014, it is awaiting further congressional authorization for its credit issuing authority. However, as a zero-subsidy federal

---

[81] See U.S. Government Accountability Office 1998, and U.S. Government Accountability Office, *Treasury's Bank Enterprise Award Program: Impact on Investments in Distressed Communities is Difficult to Determine, but Likely Not Significant*, GAO-06-824, July 2006, p. 4, at http://www.gao.gov/new.items/d06824.pdf.

[82] Laws pertaining to the Fund's Bond Guarantee program are located in 12 U.S.C. §4713a.

[83] Patient capital refers to an investment in which the investor has little expectation of earning a short-term return, in anticipation of earning more substantial returns in the longer-run.

[84] Community Development Financial Institutions Fund, "CDFI Bond Guarantee Program," at http://www.cdfifund.gov/what_we_do/programs_id.asp?programID=14.

[85] Ibid.

[86] Ibid.

[87] Catalog of Federal Domestic Assistance, "Community Development Financial Institutions Bond Guarantee Program," at https://www.cfda.gov/?s=program&mode=form&tab=step1&id=90977a236dc41c64b428744a8180642b.

program, the Bond Guarantee still requires specific authorization in the FY2013 appropriations bill to provide the initial round of bond guarantees.[88] The Senate Committee on Appropriations has provided this authorization, but the House Committee on Appropriations has not.[89] Because the program is authorized to issue no more than $1 billion in bonds per year, delays in the program's potential lending ability, under current law, has been reduced from $4 billion to $2 billion between 2010 and 2014.

Bank on USA

In his FY2011 budget request, President Obama proposed the Bank on USA program as a means to facilitate access to, and evaluate the effectiveness of, affordable, high-quality financial products, services, and education to unbanked and underbanked individuals.[90] Title 12 of the Dodd-Frank Wall Street Reform and Consumer Protection Act (P.L. 111-203) authorized the Fund to "encourage initiatives for financial products and services that are appropriate and accessible for millions of Americans who are not fully incorporated into the financial mainstream."[91]

Although the President requested more than $41 million in funding for Bank on USA for FY2012, Congress did not approve funding for the program for FY2012.[92] The Obama Administration requested $20 million for the Fund's Bank on USA-related activities for FY2013.[93] The Senate Committee on Appropriations recommended $20 million for the Bank on USA program for FY2013, whereas the House Committee on Appropriations did not recommend a specific level of funds for the program for FY2013.[94]

Policy Considerations

This section analyzes four policy considerations that may generate congressional attention, regarding the Fund's use of federal resources to promote economic development. First, it analyzes the debate on targeting development assistance toward people versus places. Second, it analyzes the debate over targeting economic development policies towards labor or capital. Third, it

---

[88] Any federal program that provides direct loans or loan guarantees is subject to Federal Credit Reform Act (FCRA) of 1990 in the Omnibus Budget Reconciliation Act of 1990 (P.L. 101-508). Sections 504 and 505 of FCRA require an annual appropriations bill to provide budget authority for new direct loan obligations incurred during the relevant fiscal year. For more information, see CRS Report R42632, *Budgetary Treatment of Federal Credit (Direct Loans and Loan Guarantees): Concepts, History, and Issues for the 112th Congress*, by James M. Bickley.

[89] U.S. Congress, House Committee on Appropriations, Financial Services and General Government Appropriations Bill, 2013, 112th Cong., 2nd sess., June 26, 2012, H.Rept. 112-550 (Washington: GPO, 2012), p. 16.; and U.S. Congress, Senate Committee on Appropriations, Financial Services and General Government Appropriations Bill, 2013, 112th Cong., 2nd sess., June 14, 2012, S.Rept. 112-177 (Washington: GPO, 2012), p. 22.

[90] Community Development Financial Institutions Fund, *FY2013 President's Budget Submission*, , p. 9, at http://www.treasury.gov/about/budget-performance/Documents/7%20-%20FY%202013%20CDFI%20CJ.pdf.

[91] Community Development Financial Institutions Fund, *FY 2013 President's Budget Submission*, p.12, at http://www.treasury.gov/about/budget-performance/Documents/7%20-%20FY%202013%20CDFI%20CJ.pdf.

[92] Ibid., p. 11.

[93] Ibid., p. 9.

[94] U.S. Congress, House Committee on Appropriations, Financial Services and General Government Appropriations Bill, 2013, 112th Cong., 2nd sess., June 26, 2012, H.Rept. 112-550 (Washington: GPO, 2012), p. 16.; and U.S. Congress, Senate Committee on Appropriations, Financial Services and General Government Appropriations Bill, 2013, 112th Cong., 2nd sess., June 14, 2012, S.Rept. 112-177 (Washington: GPO, 2012), p. 22.

---

examines whether the Fund plays a unique role in promoting economic development, or if it duplicates, compliments, or competes with the goals and activities of other federal, state, and local programs. Fourth, it examines assessments of the Fund's management.

How Effective Are Geographically Targeted Economic Development Policies?

From an economic perspective, what theoretical basis is there for the promotion of development in distressed communities? Economic theory suggests that firms and workers will locate to the most efficient and productive areas to do business in the long run, without the assistance of government policy. From this perspective, government policies, such as tax exemptions or tax expenditures, that create incentives to locate in one area at the expense of another results in net social loss of efficiency—where finite resources are not being used to produce their maximum output for the lowest cost.[95] Economic theory indicates that these policies create a distortion in the market, such that resources are directed from an area of higher potential productivity to an area of lower potential productivity.[96]

However, government policy may be economically justified if business investment in distressed communities would generate positive *externalities*.[97] Positive externalities, also known as spillover benefits, occur when the actions of one individual or firm benefit others in society. Because a given business will tend to only consider its own (private) benefit from an activity, and not the total benefit to society, too little of the positive externality-generating activity may be undertaken from society's perspective. Governments, however, may intervene through the use of taxes, subsidies, and other forms of assistance to align the interests of individual businesses with the interests of society to achieve a more economically efficient outcome.

How may government policy generate positive externalities within a community? It is possible that potential investors may invest in an underdeveloped community as long as the potential return on that investment exceeds the potential risk. If investors are not attracted to a particular community, however, government incentives may be able to change investors' perceived return and risk calculations. If this initial group of businesses is successful, due in part to the government's incentives, then they may send positive signals about potential return for other businesses that choose to locate in the community. In addition, if government incentives encourage employment in the communities, employees may feel they have more of a stake in the community and participate positively in activities outside of work. Although government incentives initially benefit particular businesses or investments, they may also allow the broader community to capture these spillover benefits.

---

[95] Economists typically view the most efficient means of production as the one that provides the most benefit at the lowest cost.

[96] Herbert G. Grubel, "Review of *Enterprise Zones: Greenlining the Inner Cities,* by Stuart M. Butler," *Journal of Economic Literature*, vol. XX (December 1982), pp. 1614-1616.

[97] A non-economic justification for a governmental role in targeted economic development policy is that these low-income communities are largely composed of minority or low-education populations. Although this argument is outside of the scope of this paper, more information on this policy justification can be found in Timothy Bartik, *Who Benefits From State and Local Economic Development Policies?* (Kalamazoo, MI: W. E. Upjohn Institute for Employment Research, 1991).

Empirical evaluations of geographically targeted economic development policies have been mixed.[98] Evaluations differ, in part, due to several factors, including the use of different evaluation criteria for economic development, different policies or sample areas used for analysis, or the use of different empirical strategies. Many of these studies are based on variations of state and local enterprise zones and federal empowerment zones. Enterprise zones typically provide certain tax incentives and regulatory relief for distressed communities, whereas federal Empowerment Zones provide certain tax exemptions and employer tax credits for hiring new employees.

Some studies have found that geographically targeted policies have a positive effect on several indicators of economic activity in the targeted area. These studies cite that these policies facilitate entrepreneurship and increase employment in the targeted area.[99] Ham et al. find that Empowerment Zone designation reduces local unemployment and poverty rates by 8.7% and 8.8%, respectively, whereas enterprise zone designation reduces local unemployment and poverty rates by 2.6% and 20%, respectively.[100] Papke's review of surveys from participants in multiple U.S. enterprise zones indicates that start-up firms average approximately 25% of new businesses within the targeted zones.[101] Rubin and Wilder's analysis of Indiana's Enterprise Zone indicates that 76% of the 1,878 jobs created between the beginning of the program in 1983 and 1986 could not be attributed to regional or sectoral growth.[102] Assuming that these residual jobs were created in large part due to policy, the researchers calculated that the creation of each of these 1,430 jobs cost taxpayers $1,372 per job, annually.[103]

On the other hand, other evaluations indicate that these policies have little effect on economic activity within the targeted area, or they do not contribute to a net increase of economic activity throughout the larger economy. These studies find that geographically targeted policies encourage some types of economic activity at the detriment of others—thus rearranging the mix of economic activity within the target area.[104] For example, Hanson and Rohlin indicate that location based-tax

---

[98] Terry F. Buss, "The Effect of State Tax Incentives on Economic Growth and Firm Location Decisions: An Overview of the Literature," *Economic Development Quarterly*, vol. 15, no. 1 (February 2001), pp. 90-105.

[99] For other studies that have found that geographically targeted development policies have positive effects on economic activity in the target area, see Stephen Billings, "Do Enterprise Zones Work? An Analysis at the Borders," *Public Finance Review*, vol. 37, no. 1 (2008), pp. 68-93, and Douglas Krupka and Douglas Noonan, "Empowerment Zones, Neighborhood Change, and Owner Occupied Housing," *Regional Science and Urban Economics*, vol. 39, no. 4 (2009), pp. 386-396.

[100] John C. Ham et al., "Government Programs Can Improve Local Labor Markets: Evidence from State Enterprise Zones, Federal Empowerment Zones, and Federal Enterprise Communities," *Journal of Public Economics*, vol. 95, no. 7-8 (July 2011), pp. 779-797.

[101] Leslie Papke, "What Do We Know About Enterprise Zones?," in *Tax Policy and the Economy*, ed. James Poterba, vol. 7 (Cambridge, MA: MIT Press, 1993), pp. 32-72.

[102] Barry M. Rubin and Margaret G. Wilder, "Urban Enterprise Zones: Employment Impacts and Fiscal Incentives," *Journal of the American Planning Association*, vol. 55, no. 4 (Autumn 1989), pp. 418-431.

[103] Rubin and Wilder's cost estimates are among the lowest in the literature. In Ladd's review of six studies of enterprise zones, the basic annual cost estimates of various programs ranged from $1,633 to $53,507 per job, depending on methodology used to calculate costs. Bartik's (1992) review of 57 studies of state and local tax incentives found annual cost estimates ranging from $2,000 to $11,000 per job. See Helen F. Ladd, "Spatially Targeted Economic Development Strategies: Do They Work?," *Cityscape*, vol. 1, no. 1 (August 1994), pp. 193-218, and Timothy J. Bartik, "The Effects of State and Local Taxes on Economic Development: A Review of Recent Research," *Economic Development Quarterly*, vol. 6, no. 1 (1992), pp. 102-111.

[104] For studies that have found that geographically targeted development policies have little or no positive effects on economic activity in the target area, see Marlon Boarnet and William Bogart, "Enterprise Zones and Employment: Evidence from New Jersey," *Journal of Urban Economics*, vol. 40, no. 2 (1996), pp. 198-215; Danielle Bondonio and (continued...)

---

incentives have a positive effect on the firm location in industries that benefit the most from the tax incentives, but net growth in new establishments is offset by declines or slower growth in other industries that are less likely to utilize the tax incentives.[105]

In addition, some studies indicate that geographically targeted policies may shift activity from a comparative area toward the targeted zone, rather than create new economic activity. For example, Gurley-Calvez et al. find that the NMTC may have led to an increase in corporate investment within the targeted areas, but did not lead to a net increase in corporate investment.[106] These authors conclude that the NMTC might encourage investment to shift from one low-income community (LIC) to another close substitute, as some corporate investors might already be investing in LICs to fulfill Community Reinvestment Act requirements.[107]

The effect of geographically targeted economic development policies on local property prices is also an area of contention among researchers.[108] From a theoretical perspective, government incentives to increase the supply of affordable property increase the demand for that property. That increase in demand drives rents higher. If local residents do not benefit from the increase in economic activity, then higher property values may encourage those with lower incomes to move out of the community.[109]

Given the lack of consensus among researchers on the effectiveness of geographically targeted economic policies, policymakers may opt to more narrowly define the core objective of *development*. At its core, the debate is a question of whether development policies should help people or places. If the primary objective is to improve business and employment opportunities relative to other areas, then these policies might be effective. If the primary objective of such policies are to create new jobs, then the effect of these policies may be limited. If policymakers wish to help the poor, then it might be asked why should government assistance only be extended to the poor living in distressed communities (as opposed to the poor living in non-distressed

---

(...continued)

John Engberg, "Enterprise Zones and Local Employment: Evidence from the States' Programs," *Regional Science and Urban Economics*, vol. 30, no. 5 (2000), pp. 519-549; Robert Greenbaum and John Engberg, "The Impact of State Enterprise Zones on Urban Manufacturing Establishments," *Journal of Policy Analysis and Management*, vol. 23, no. 2 (2004), pp. 315-339; and David Neumark and Jed Kolko, "Do Enterprise Zones Create Jobs? Evidence from California's Enterprise Zone Program," *Journal of Urban Economics*, vol. 68, no. 1 (2010), pp. 1-19.

[105] Andrew Hanson and Shawn Rohlin, "Do Location-Based Tax Incentives Attract New Business Establishments?," *Journal of Regional Science*, vol. 51, no. 3 (2011), pp. 427-449.

[106] Tami Gurley-Calvez et al., "An Analysis of the New Markets Tax Credit," *Public Finance Review*, vol. 37, no. 4 (July 2009), pp. 371-398.

[107] The Community Reinvestment Act (CRA), passed by Congress in 1977, encourages financial institutions to help meet their communities' needs through safe and sound lending practices and by providing retail banking and community development services. The Federal Reserve System, the Federal Deposit Insurance Corporation, the Office of the Comptroller of the Currency, and the Office of Thrift Supervision are responsible for enforcing the CRA. Banks are evaluated for their CRA performance according to various criteria. See Federal Reserve Bank of Atlanta, "Standards Used to Evaluate Your Bank's CRA Performance,"at http://www.frbatlanta.org/pubs/cra/standards_used_to_evaluate_your_banks_cra_performance.cfm.

[108] For studies that have model the effects of geographically targeted development policies on property values in the target area, see Douglas Krupka and Douglas Noonan, "Empowerment Zones, Neighborhood Change, and Owner Occupied Housing," *Regional Science and Urban Economics*, vol. 39, no. 4 (2009), pp. 386-396 and Andrew Hanson, "Local Employment, Poverty, and Property Value Effects of Geographically-Targeted Tax Incentives: An Instrumental Variables Approach," *Regional Science and Urban Economics*, vol. 39, no. 6 (November 2009), pp. 721-731.

[109] Andrew Hanson and Shawn Rohlin, "The Effect of Location Based Tax Incentives on Establishment Location and Employment Across Industry Sectors," *Public Finance Review*, vol. 39, no. 2 (March 2011), pp. 195-225.

communities)? Each standard for evaluation implies a different set of metrics and results in a different set of trade-offs.

Should Economic Development Policies Target Capital or Labor?

Assuming that geographically targeted policies can positively affect economic development within the intended community, then what type of benefit is most effective? Policies can provide a benefit related to labor costs, capital costs, or both (i.e., total costs). In other words, should development policies target workers, business owners, or both?

When a geographically targeted subsidy is applied to one of these two factors of production, economic theory suggests that two behavioral responses occur. The first response is that total output (i.e., economic activity) increases. This increase in total output increases the use of both capital and labor, to some degree. Economists label this the *output effect* of production. The second response is a *substitution effect*, whereby firms use one factor of production at the detriment of the other. The net effect of the output effect and substitution effect determines the total effect of the policy. In other words, the total effect reflects whether the policy benefits labor more than capital, or vice versa.

For example, a labor subsidy, such as a payroll tax credit for hiring a worker, provided within a particular area will encourage labor-intensive firms to locate within that same area. All firms (whether attracted by the labor subsidy or already operating in the area) will tend, in addition to expanding operations, to substitute their use of labor for capital. If the objective of the labor subsidy is to promote employment, then the substitution effect (the use of more labor, relative to capital) reinforces the benefits of the output effect (the use of more labor, due to expanded operation). In other words, the policy is expected to result in a net increase in employment.

By contrast, a capital subsidy, such as tax deductions for capital investments, provided within a particular area will encourage capital-intensive firms to locate within the area. All firms (whether attracted by the capital subsidy or already operating in the area) will tend, in addition to expanding operations, to substitute their use of capital for labor. If the objective of the capital subsidy is to promote employment, then the substitution effect (the use of more capital, relative to labor) offsets the benefits of the output effect (the use of more labor, due to expanded operation). Moreover, if the substitution effect is more powerful than the output effect, a capital subsidy may end up *decreasing* employment in the area.[110] In this instance, the net effect of the capital subsidy is less employment in the area than before the policy.

Policies that relate to total costs may balance the trade-off between the promotion of capital or labor in the targeted area. If producers are indifferent between using labor or capital, then a policy that provides equally weighted incentives toward the employment of labor and capital will result in a positive income effect, with no substitution effect. However, if producers use relative factor price differentials to inform the mix of capital and labor they employ, then the result of a policy that relates to total costs will depend on the strength and direction of the substitution effect.

Studies indicate that geographically targeted tax incentives for business owners (e.g., the NMTC) have a positive, but limited effect in increasing the economic well-being of other individuals

---

[110] CRS Report 92-476 S *Enterprise Zones: The Design of Tax Incentives*, by Jane G. Gravelle (out of print; available by request) models this possible effect of geographically targeted tax incentives.

living within the target area. Bartik's review of 57 empirical studies on the effect of state and local preferential tax incentives for employers in a state or metropolitan area found that 57% of the studies found at least one statistically significant effect on generating development in the target area.[111] Bartik found that the average measure of responsiveness, or elasticities, or change between tax measures and economic activity in a targeted state or metropolitan area range from -0.25 across all studies to -0.51 for studies that include statistical controls for both public service and fixed effects. In other words, the study concluded that a 10% reduction in all taxes within a particular geographic zone would generate a 2.5% to 5.1% increase in economic activity within the same zone.

Do the Fund's Programs Duplicate Other Government Efforts?

There has been growing legislative interest in identifying duplicative federal programs, as some Members of Congress have become concerned about the size or efficient management of federal budgetary resources. GAO defines duplicative programs as federal programs that overlap with the goals or activities of other federal, state, or local policies.[112]

Some say that the Fund's programs duplicate other federal, state, local, and private-sector efforts to increase economic development in distressed and low-income communities. The Fund's website contains a guide that provides a list of possible financing sources for CDFIs.[113] At the federal level, various programs exist as possible sources of finance for CDFIs. These programs are managed by executive agencies, such as USDA, SBA, HHS, the Departments of Housing and Urban Development (HUD), Interior, Treasury, and Commerce. Based on this variety of possible funding sources for CDFIs, the Office of Management and Budget (OMB), under President George W. Bush, said that the Fund's core CDFI program was *not unique*, as several states administer similar programs and CDFIs can use private-sector equity investment to accomplish activities that they would otherwise accomplish with the Fund's awards.[114]

In addition, the NMTC is not the only tax incentive designed to encourage economic development in distressed communities. The Senate Committee on the Budget Print on Tax Expenditures lists several other tax incentives that are meant to achieve similar goals as the NMTC. These incentives provide short-term development assistance (e.g., disaster relief provisions), enhance tribal area development, and encourage business and capital investment in target communities.[115] The Bush era's OMB also stated that the NMTC was not unique because

---

[111] Bartik (1992).

[112] U.S. Government Accountability Office, *Opportunities to Reduce Duplication, Overlap and Fragmentation, Achieve Savings, and Enhance Revenue*, GAO-12-342SP, February 28, 2012, p.1, http://www.gao.gov/products/GAO-12-342SP.

[113] Community Development Financial Institutions Fund, *Financial Resources Catalog*, June 11, 2012, at http://www.cdfifund.gov/what_we_do/resources/Financial%20Resources%20Catalogue%20PDF.pdf.

[114] The Office of Management and Budget (OMB) under President George W. Bush maintained ExpectMore.gov, a website that listed performance evaluations and issued budgetary recommendations across executive branch agencies. OMB under President Bush implemented the Program Assessment Rating Tool (PART), as a means to assess the effectiveness of federal programs and help inform management actions, budget requests, and legislative proposals. For OMB's last PART assessment of the Fund and the NMTC, see Office of Management and Budget, *FY 2009 Budget Performance: Community Development Financial Institutions Fund*, pp. 15-16, at http://www.treasury.gov/about/budget-performance/Documents/CJ%20FY09-CDFI.pdf.

[115] See U.S. Congress, Senate Committee on the Budget, *Tax Expenditures: Compendium of Background Material on Individual Provisions*, committee print, prepared by the Congressional Research Service, 111th Cong., 2nd sess., (continued...)

other federal, state, and local tax credit programs are available through agencies, such as HUD and Commerce's Economic Development Agency.[116]

On the other hand, there are those that believe that the Fund plays a unique or complementary role to the programs mentioned above. First, Fund supporters most commonly argue that community lenders are ready and willing to fill financing gaps, but they often struggle to find the amount of capital and liquidity they need to meet loan demand in distressed communities.[117] Although certain CDFIs may be eligible for similar forms of assistance from other federal programs (e.g., guaranteed loans from SBA), the Fund's limitations to activities in distressed communities allows CDFIs to compete with other entities that face similar economic, environmental, and geographic challenges. Second, Fund programs have supported alternatives to predatory lending institutions in distressed communities—notably in tribal communities.[118] Third, some argue that the Fund's programs complement, not compete with, the goals and programs of other federal initiatives. For example, former-Assistant Secretary for Financial Institutions Michael Barr testified before the House Committee on Financial Services that funding for the Community Reinvestment Act encourages more entities to invest in CDFIs.[119]

In contrast to the assessment by the Bush era's OMB, some say that the Fund provides incentives for activity that private-sector investors would not otherwise engage in. For example, the Fund enables more CDFIs to provide affordable, critical-gap financing for businesses.[120] In other words, the Fund encourages CDFIs to provide short-term loans to businesses or homebuyers to cover financial obligations in the meantime, while that borrower secures sufficient funds to make a full payment or find a more stable financing scheme. In addition, CDFIs also provide technical assistance and training to borrowers to reduce default risk. For these reasons, some representatives from national banking chains argue that CDFIs complement traditional banking products in distressed and LICs and help these financial markets operate more efficiently.[121]

Is the Fund Managed Effectively?

Concerns over the Fund's management primarily involve questions over the transparency and consistency of the Fund's award evaluation processes. In March 1997, as a result of complaints about the selection process used in the first round of grants announced in July 1996,

---

(...continued)

December 2010, S.Prt.111-58 (Washington: GPO, 2002), pp. 566-599.

[116] Office of Management and Budget, *FY 2009 Budget Performance: Community Development Financial Institutions Fund*, pp. 15-16, at http://www.treasury.gov/about/budget-performance/Documents/CJ%20FY09-CDFI.pdf.

[117] U.S. Congress, House Committee on Financial Services, *Community Development Financial Institutions (CDFIs): Their Unique Role and Challenges Serving Lower-Income, Underserved, and Minority Communities*, 111th Cong., 2nd sess., March 9, 2010, 111-106 (Washington: GPO, 2010), p.99.

[118] U.S. Congress, Senate Committee on Indian Affairs, *Predatory Lending in Indian Country*, 110th Cong., 2nd sess., June 5, 2008, 110-484 (Washington: GPO, 2008), p. 13.

[119] U.S. Congress, House Committee on Financial Services, *Community Development Financial Institutions (CDFIs): Their Unique Role and Challenges Serving Lower-Income, Underserved, and Minority Communities*, 111th Cong., 2nd sess., March 9, 2010, 111-106 (Washington: GPO, 2010), p.7.

[120] Federal Reserve Bank of Richmond, "Community Development Financial Institutions: A Unique Partnership for Banks," *Community Development Special Issue*, 2011, p.2, at http://www.richmondfed.org/community_development/announcements/2011/pdf/cdfi-special-2011.pdf.

[121] Ibid.

Representative Spencer Bachus, chairman of the General Oversight and Investigations Subcommittee (the Subcommittee) of the House Committee on Banking and Financial Services, requested information about management practices at the Fund from Treasury. At Chairman Bachus's request, the majority staff of the subcommittee published a report that reviewed the management practices at the Fund. The majority staff report indicated that the Fund had failed to employ an objective scoring system in selecting award winners in its first round of allocations, and that the director and deputy director of the Fund had participated in making awards to firms with that they had been previously associated.[122] Chairman Bachus asserted that the Fund's award evaluation process had been politically motivated by the White House, naming Shorebank of Chicago, Illinois, and several other community development organizations affiliated with Shorebank among the award-recipients.[123] The majority staff report also indicated that, when it made its first round of awards, the Fund did not follow the recommendations of Treasury's Office of Inspector General (OIG) to adopt draft procedures for a numerical scoring system, a procedure similar to that used by other federal grant programs to ensure objectivity in the review process.[124]

In August 1997, Treasury Secretary Robert Rubin replied to a request from Chairman Leach of the Senate Banking Committee by providing a detailed outline of procedural and organization reforms to be implemented by the Fund in its 1997 funding round.[125] These reforms included the development of selection criteria, a conflict of interest policy for Fund reviewers, and other tools and procedures to encourage consistent evaluation of award applications. Secretary Rubin's letter also announced the resignations of the Fund's director and deputy director. The subcommittee's staff conducted a review of the Fund's second round of awards in 1997. Although the majority staff report recommended further actions to enhance the fund's management and review processes, subcommittee staff concluded that the Fund "appeared to make great strides in documenting the grant process."[126]

In addition, some have expressed concern about the Fund's ability to develop clear performance goals. In 1998, GAO released a report on the Fund's performance.[127] GAO acknowledged that assessing the Fund's performance was difficult, as the Fund's authorizing legislation provides limited guidance for evaluating performance measures and staffing limits delayed the Fund's ability to develop mandated monitoring and evaluation systems.[128] GAO stated that until the Fund identifies the types of data needed to monitor and evaluate awardees and incorporates these data

---

[122] U.S. Congress, House Committee on Banking and Financial Services, Subcommittee on General Oversight and Investigations, *Review of Management Practice at the Treasury Department's Community Development Financial Institutions Fund*, committee print, prepared by Majority Staff, 105th Cong., 2nd sess., June 1998, 105-2 (Washington: GPO, 1998), pp. 1-9.

[123] Ibid., p. (v) and 9. Note 1 on p. 9 details the majority staff's views on the connections between Shorebank, its affiliates, First Lady Hillary Clinton, and President Clinton.

[124] Ibid., p. 4.

[125] Ibid., p. 95.

[126] Ibid., p. 96.

[127] Section 112(c)(3) of the Riegle Act mandated the Comptroller General (Director of GAO) to submit to the President and the Congress a study evaluating the structure, governance, and performance of the Fund. However, GAO, in consultation with the four congressional committees that the report was submitted to, only examined the Fund's performance measures in its 1998 study, due to a concurrent audit of structure and governance issues being conducted by Treasury's Inspector General. See the correspondence of Judy A. England-Joseph, GAO Director of Housing and Community Development Issues to Congressional Committees in U.S. General Accounting Office, *Community Development Financial Institutions Fund Can Improve Its Systems to Measure, Monitor, and Evaluate Awardees' Performance*, GAO/RCED-98-225, July 1998, at http://www.gao.gov/assets/160/156245.pdf.

[128] Ibid., p.6.

needs in a formal system, it will be hampered in its ability to report on its progress toward achieving its stated goals and objectives.[129] GAO also noted that the Fund could fulfill its strategic goal to coordinate its strategies with other Treasury bureaus and agencies with similar missions (e.g., HUD and the SBA).[130] According to GAO, interagency coordination is important for ensuring that crosscutting programs are mutually reinforcing and efficiently implemented. Therefore, the Fund's strategic plan would be strengthened if it identified and incorporated some descriptions of other agencies' programs with similar missions and discussed their influence on the Fund's strategic objectives.[131]

Some Members of Congress have expressed concern regarding the lack of CDFIs that serve U.S. territories and rural communities.[132] However, a 2012 GAO report concluded that the policies and procedures of the CDFI and NMTC Programs help ensure that awards and allocations generally are proportionate to the numbers of qualified applicants that serve metropolitan and nonmetropolitan areas.[133] In addition, some Members of Congress have expressed interest in the performance of CDFIs compared with their non-CDFI, peers.[134]

In addition, some Members of Congress have raised concerns over the use of funds from the Troubled Asset Relief Program (TARP) for assistance to CDFIs. President Obama authorized a program that made certified CDFIs eligible to receive capital investments at a discounted dividend, with the intent of increasing the supply of credit to community banks.[135] Some maintained that TARP's temporary funds were not intended to target regional banks, and the program functionally resulted in a bypass of the typical appropriations process for the Fund.[136]

[129] Ibid., p.63.

[130] Ibid., p.62.

[131] Ibid.

[132] U.S. Congress, House Committee on Appropriations, *Financial Services and General Government Appropriations Bill, 2013*, 112th Cong., 2nd sess., June 26, 2012, H.Rept. 112-550 (Washington: GPO, 2012), p. 16.

[133] U.S. Government Accountability Office, *Community Development Financial Institutions and New Markets Tax Credit Programs in Metropolitan and Nonmetropolitan Areas*, GAO-12-547R, April 26, 2012, p. 4, http://www.gao.gov/assets/600/590432.pdf.

[134] U.S. Congress, House Committee on Financial Services, *Community Development Financial Institutions (CDFIs): Their Unique Role and Challenges Serving Lower-Income, Underserved, and Minority Communities*, 111th Cong., 2nd sess., March 9, 2010, 111-106 (Washington: GPO, 2010), p. 19 and 24.

[135] U.S. Department of the Treasury, "Obama Administration Announces Enhancements for TARP Initiative for Community Development Financial Institutions," press release, February 3, 2010, at http://www.cdfifund.gov/docs/2010/cdfi/Obama-Administration-Announces-Enhancements-Tarp-Initiative-for-Community-Dev-Fin-Inst.pdf.

[136] U.S. Congress, House Committee on Financial Services, *Community Development Financial Institutions (CDFIs): Their Unique Role and Challenges Serving Lower-Income, Underserved, and Minority Communities*, 111th Cong., 2nd sess., March 9, 2010, 111-106 (Washington: GPO, 2010), p. 8.

Appendix A. Inactive programs

Capital Magnet Fund

The Housing and Economic Recovery Act (HERA) of 2008 (P.L. 110-289) established the Capital Magnet Fund (CMF) for CDFIs and other nonprofits to expand financing for the development, rehabilitation and purchase of affordable housing and economic development projects in distressed communities.[137] Through the CMF the Fund provided competitively awarded grants to CDFIs and qualified nonprofit housing organizations. CMF awards could be used to finance affordable housing activities as well as related economic development activities and community service facilities. Awardees were able to use financing tools, such as loan loss reserves, loan funds, risk-sharing loans, and loan guarantees, to produce eligible activities whose aggregate costs are at least 10 times the size of the award amount.[138]

Three types of organizations were eligible to apply for a CMF award. An organization applying for a CMF Award had to either (1) be certified as a CDFI by the Fund; (2) have an application for CDFI certification pending with the CDFI Fund, provided such application was submitted prior to the due date specified in the applicable notice of funds availability; or (3) be a nonprofit organization having as one of its principal purposes the development or management of affordable housing.[139]

As authorized in HERA, CMF was to receive funding via a set-aside from government-sponsored enterprises (GSEs), such as Fannie Mae and Freddie Mac. However, such contributions have been suspended indefinitely. The GSEs never made contributions to the CMF, as was originally expected under HERA, due to their financial condition and status under conservatorships.[140] Instead, the Consolidation Appropriations Act, 2010 (P.L. 111-117) appropriated $80 million in initial funding for the CMF for FY2010.[141] Funding for the CMF was discontinued for FY2011.

The Fund awarded grants to 23 CDFIs and qualified nonprofit housing organizations serving in FY2010.[142] In FY2013, the Fund will provide performance results from the initial round of CMF recipients. The Fund received a total of 230 applications requesting $1 billion for the FY2010 CMF funding round.[143]

---

[137] Laws pertaining to the CMF are located in 46 U.S.C. §1807.

[138] Community Development Financial Institutions Fund, "Capital Magnet Fund," June 8, 2012, at http://www.cdfifund.gov/what_we_do/programs_id.asp?programID=11.

[139] Ibid.

[140] U.S. Congress, House Committee on Financial Services, Subcommittee on Capital Markets and Government Sponsored Enterprises, *Transparency, Transition, and Taxpayer Protection: More Steps to End the GSE Bailout*, 112th Cong., 1st sess., May 25, 2011, 112-33 (Washington: GPO, 2011), p. 10.

[141] Department of the Treasury, *Community Development Financial Institutions Fund - Agency Financial Report FY 2011*, November 16, 2011, p. 8, at http://www.cdfifund.gov/news_events/ CDFI%20Fund%20FY%202011%20Agency%20Financial%20Report%20FINAL%2011%2016%2011.pdf.

[142] U.S. Department of the Treasury, *Community Development Financial Institutions Fund: Agency Financial Report FY 2012*, November 2011, at http://www.cdfifund.gov/news_events/ CDFI%20Fund%20FY%202011%20Agency%20Financial%20Report%20FINAL%2011%2016%2011.pdf.

[143] Department of the Treasury, *Community Development Financial Institutions Fund - Agency Financial Report FY 2011*, November 16, 2011, p. 30, at http://www.cdfifund.gov/news_events/ (continued...)

Financial Education and Counseling Pilot Program

The Financial Education and Counseling (FEC) pilot program provided grants through FY2010 to organizations that provided financial education and counseling services to prospective homebuyers. The goals of the FEC pilot program were to increase the financial knowledge and decision-making capabilities of prospective homebuyers, assist prospective buyers to plan for major purchases, and provide information on how to improve credit scores. Certified CDFIs, a HUD-approved housing counseling agency, credit union, or government entity could request FEC funding for administrative expenses for FEC-related programs.[144]

Section 1132 of HERA of 2008 (P.L. 110-289) authorized the Secretary of the Treasury to create FEC pilot programs. For FY2009, Congress appropriated $2 million to the Fund for the FEC program.[145] Treasury selected five organizations to receive $400,000 for their services toward the mission of the program.[146] In FY2010, Congress appropriated $4.15 million, of which $3.15 million was designated for an eligible organization in Hawaii.[147]

A 2011 GAO report concluded that Treasury's process for selecting FEC grantees was applied consistently using established criteria. In 2010, the four grantees served a combined total of 311 clients.[148] However, GAO could not meaningfully assess the impact of the program or the effectiveness of individual grantees because grantees had been providing services under the FEC program for less than a year.[149]

(...continued)

CDFI%20Fund%20FY%202011%20Agency%20Financial%20Report%20FINAL%2011%2016%2011.pdf.

[144] For further details about the objective and eligibility criteria of the FEC pilot program, see Community Development Financial Institutions Fund, "Financial Education and Counseling Pilot Program," June 5, 2012, at http://www.cdfifund.gov/what_we_do/programs_id.asp?programID=8.

[145] U..S. Department of Treasury Office of Inspector General, *Audit of the Community Development Financial Institutions Fund's Fiscal Years 2010 and 2009 Financial Statements*, Department of the Treasury, OIG-11-024, November 15, 2010, at http://www.treasury.gov/about/organizational-structure/ig/Documents/oig11024%20%28CDFI%20Financials%20FY%2010%29.pdf.

[146] U.S. Government Accountability Office, *Financial Education and Counseling*, GAO-11-737R, July 27, 2011, p.2, at http://www.gao.gov/new.items/d11737r.pdf.

[147] Ibid.

[148] According to the 2011 GAO report, one grantee, the New Hampshire Housing Finance Authority, used their FEC award to develop an interactive financial education website that had not been launched when GAO reports were due.

[149] Ibid.

Appendix B. Certified Native CDFIs

Table B-1. Certified Native CDFIs, by State

State	Certified Native CDFIs
Hawaii	11
Oklahoma	10
Alaska	6
Arizona	6
South Dakota	6
Minnesota	5
Montana	4
California	3
Colorado	3
New Mexico	3
Washington	3
Wisconsin	3
Michigan	2
North Carolina	2
Maine	1
Mississippi	1
North Dakota	1
Oregon	1
Wyoming	1
Total	**72**

Source: Community Development Financial Institutions Fund, http://www.cdfifund.gov/docs/certification/cdfi/
CDFI%20List%20-%2007-31-12.xls

Note: CDFI counts are as of July 31, 2012.

Author Contact Information

Sean Lowry
Analyst in Public Finance
slowry@crs.loc.gov, 7-9154

www.ingramcontent.com/pod-product-compliance
Lightning Source LLC
Chambersburg PA
CBHW061009200526
45171CB00009B/551

* 9 7 8 1 4 8 0 1 5 1 6 9 7 *